Tell Me Why

WHY?

The Wind Blows

Tamra B. Orr

Published in the United States of America by Cherry Lake Publishing
Ann Arbor, Michigan
www.cherrylakepublishing.com

Content Adviser: Jack Williams, Fellow of the American Meteorological Society
Reading Adviser: Marla Conn, ReadAbility, Inc

Photo Credits: © Photobank gallery/Shutterstock Images, cover, 1; © Christian Delbert/Shutterstock
Images, cover, 1; © Gregory Johnston/Shutterstock Images, cover, 1; © I Love Travel/Shutterstock Images,
5; © EpicStockMedia/Shutterstock Images, 7; © T.W. van Urk/Shutterstock Images, 9; © Paul Aniszewski/
Shutterstock Images, 11; © Michael Ciranni/Shutterstock Images, 13; © topseller/Shutterstock Images, 15;
© MarcelClemens/Shutterstock Images, 17; © welcomia/Shutterstock Images, 19; © CroMary/Shutterstock
Images, 21

Library of Congress Cataloging-in-Publication Data

CIP data has been filed and is available at catalog.loc.gov.

Cherry Lake Publishing would like to acknowledge the work of The Partnership for 21st Century Skills.
Please visit www.p21.org for more information.

Printed in the United States of America.
Corporate Graphics

Table of Contents

A Windy Campground

"Mom, did you see that?" Kinsey shouted. "Our tent was almost completely flattened!" Luckily they weren't in it.

The weather at the campsite had been sunny and warm. As it got darker, a cool wind started blowing. Huge pine trees surrounded the campground. The treetops swayed back and forth in the wind as if they were dancing.

Their tent stood down in a valley. Every few minutes, the wind rocketed through and squashed their tent to the ground.

Campers often stake a tent to the ground so that it doesn't get blown away by the wind.

"We'd better add a few extra stakes to the tent, to keep it from taking off," Mom suggested.

They secured the tent just in time. The wind suddenly rushed through the valley with a roar. They huddled around the campfire as it dipped and flickered with the wind.

"Mom," Kinsey finally said. "I don't get it. Why does the wind blow in the first place?"

"Let's grab our extra sweaters, and I'll tell you," Mom said, chuckling. "It might not be the usual campfire story, but it fits the situation!"

The wind can be strong in the mountains.

Sunshine, Temperature, and Pressure

"Wind is the motion of air across the earth's surface," Mom explained. "We can't see it moving, but we sure can feel it." The tent **billowed** as the wind hit it from different directions.

"Scientists use an instrument called an **anemometer** to measure the speed of the wind," Mom said. "It looks a little like a **weather vane.**"

Most anemometers have tiny cups on a small rod that sticks up into the air. How fast they spin shows wind speed. A weather vane connected to the spinning cups shows the direction the wind is coming from.

An anemometer measures the speed of the wind.

The sun causes the wind to blow. Its hot rays shine down on the earth, bringing warmth. But the planet's surface is not the same all over. Some parts are covered in long mountain ranges. Some parts are valleys. Some have huge sections of sand, while others are covered in huge oceans. Each area absorbs the sun's heat differently.

"Think of the pool in summer," Mom explained. "The sidewalks are hot, while the water surface is cool."

The areas that absorb the sun's **radiation** the most get hot. Warm air is lighter, so it begins to rise. This creates a **low pressure** area. On the other hand, cool air sinks. Sinking air creates a **high pressure**

The amount of sunlight can affect the wind in a specific place.

area. Air always flows from high pressure to low. So as the warm air rises, cool air rushes in to take its place. That movement creates wind.

This accounts for some winds, Mom said, but not all of them. "You've seen the **meteorologist** on Channel 4 talk about **jet streams**, the fast winds high up in the sky," she said. "Sometimes the sides of a jet stream squeeze together, pushing air down to create high pressure on the ground. At other times a jet stream spreads out and pulls air up, creating low pressure on the ground."

MAKE A GUESS!

What do you think is the biggest danger from strong winds? How are powerful winds different at the coast?

Wind often knocks down trees during storms.

13

Another Look at Highs and Lows

"I don't really get what pressure has to do with creating wind," Kinsey admitted.

"Imagine a balloon you've poked with a needle," Mom said. "As the air escapes, it creates wind. That wind is blowing from the higher pressure inside the balloon to the lower pressure outside."

Wind flows directly from high pressure to low over short distances. But sometimes the difference in the pressure covers a very large area. Then the wind is also affected by the rotation, or turning, of the earth. This is known as the **Coriolis effect**.

Hot air balloons work similarly to how a party balloon works when you poke a hole in it. But they're much bigger and more controlled!

The constant spinning of the earth causes the wind to swirl instead of move in a straight line. So the wind curves as it travels from one place to the next. "So a valley like this one gets wind that is swirling instead of moving straight," Mom said.

The speed of wind is often measured by the Beaufort Wind Scale. It sorts wind into 12 **categories**, ranging from "Calm" to "Hurricane."

"Let's say this wind is about 20 miles an hour," Mom said. "The scale would call it a Fresh Breeze."

"In that case," Kinsey said, "I'm ready for 'no breeze'!"

ASK QUESTIONS!

What do the terms *chinook* and *nor'easter* refer to? Go online with an adult and learn more.

The way the earth spins affects the patterns of the wind.

Putting the Wind to Use

As they ate breakfast the next morning, Kinsey felt the hot sun on her shoulders, but also a cool breeze. She thought of something else. "I bet wind helps to move warm and cool air around the planet!"

"Exactly," Mom agreed. "Wind carries some of the heat away. It also carries seeds from one place to another. What else do you think wind might do?"

"It helps windmills create electricity," Kinsey said.

Wind farms like this one use wind to produce electricity. Why is using wind for energy considered a good idea for the planet?

These California windmills produce electricity.

"True," Mom said. "But you missed one other thing that wind does." She went to the back of the truck and pulled out a bright red kite.

"The wind makes kites come alive," she said with a grin. "Now, let's go put this wind to good use!"

*Beaches often have a lot of wind, which is helpful
for flying kites.*

Think About It

In Asia and parts of Africa, communities experience seasonal winds called monsoons. These winds bring heavy rain during the summer. How do you think that affects the people living there? Go online to find out more.

The highest wind gust ever recorded in the United States was on April 12, 1934, on top of Mount Washington in New Hampshire. It only lasted seconds, but it hit 231 miles (372 kilometers) per hour. What might happen during a wind that strong?

Glossary

anemometer (an-uh-MAH-meh-ter) an instrument for measuring the speed of wind

billowed (BIL-ohd) bulged or swelled out, especially when pushed by the wind

categories (KAT-uh-gor-eez) groups of things that have certain characteristics in common

Coriolis effect (kor-ee-OH-liss ih-FEKT) the rotation of the earth appearing to change the direction of wind

high pressure (HYE PRESH-ur) a mass of cool, dry air that tends to bring fair weather and light winds

jet streams (JET streemz) very strong currents of wind, usually found between 4 and 9 miles above the earth's surface

low pressure (LOH PRESH-ur) a mass of warm, moist air that tends to bring storms and strong winds

meteorologist (meet-tee-uh-RAH-luh-jist) an expert in the study of the earth's atmosphere

radiation (ray-dee-AY-shuhn) energy released as waves, as from the sun

weather vane (WETH-ur vayn) a pointer that swings around on a pole to show which way the wind is blowing

Find Out More

Books:

Doeden, Matt. *Finding Out About Wind Energy*. Minneapolis: Lerner Publications, 2014.

Friedman, Mark. *What Does It Do? Windmill*. Ann Arbor, MI: Cherry Lake Publishing, 2012.

Web Sites:

Kids Ahead: Wind Energy Activities
http://kidsahead.com/subjects/2-wind-energy/activities
Here you'll find all types of wind energy experiments.

You Tube: Bill Nye the Science Guy on Wind
https://www.youtube.com/watch?v=uBqohRu2RRk
Bill Nye the Science Guy discusses wind in this two-minute video.

Index

About the Author

Tamra B. Orr is a full-time author living in the Pacific Northwest. She is a mom to four, a graduate of Ball State University, and the author of more than 375 books for readers of all ages. She lives in Oregon and loves to go camping. Her favorite nights are camping when the wind is blowing hard and the tent is rattling around.